the guide to owning a
Brittany

Stacy Kennedy

The Publisher wishes to acknowledge the following owners of the dogs in this book, including: Wendy Archinal, Michael and Lisa Bruzzone, Joan Comfort, Elude Archuleta-Cressler, Cindy Ford, Jenelle Larson, Linda McCartney, Susan B. Peckham, Frances N. Phillips, Sherri Thayer, Bouty Thierry, Karen Wagner, Betsy Wallace, Michael Zollo.

T.F.H. Publications, Inc.
One TFH Plaza
Third and Union Avenues
Neptune City, NJ 07753

ISBN 0-7938-2122-2

Printed and bound in the United States of America

Printed and Distributed by T.F.H. Publications, Inc.
Neptune City, NJ

Contents

History of the Brittany

The Brittany, or Brittany Spaniel, as it is known in other parts of the world, was developed around the 1850s in France. Early land spaniels were crossed with setters in the Bretagne region of France. It was from the breed's area of development that the Brittany derived its name.

Just after the turn of the century, Major P. Gran-Chavin, a Calvary officer and veterinarian assigned to the Bretagne region, wrote of the many small spaniels he saw. The dogs, he said, had short tails or no tails at all and rather short ears for the spaniel breeds. He described their color as white-orange, white-liver, and white-black, and also reported seeing some tricolors as well. In 1910, M. Le Comte Le Conteux de Canteleu drew up his chart of the French breeds. Here we find first mention of "Chien de Bretagne," first known as the "Dog of Brittany" and later as the "Brittany Spaniel."

THE BRITTANY IN NORTH AMERICA

The first Brittanys were brought to North America in 1928 by Senor Juan Pagibet of Villa Obregon, who resided near Vera Cruz, Mexico. Louis A. Thebaud imported Brittany Spaniels into the US in 1933. Upon Mr. Thebaud's request, the French Kennel Club sent him the "Standard of Perfection" for the breed in July of 1934.

The American Kennel Club (AKC) recognized the breed in August of 1934, but did not approve the standard until March of 1935 after an acceptable translation had been completed. The first Brittany litter known to have been born in the US was that of Gilda de Causses, a bitch that was mated to Douglas de l'Odet. The puppies were born in June of 1935. The Brittany Spaniel Club of North America was founded in 1936 and received official membership with the AKC in September of 1936. There were 11 Brittanys registered with the AKC in that year.

In April of 1935, the first official placing of a Brittany in a field trial held in the United States occurred—Franche du Cosquerou achieved the distinction of placing third in the Jockey Hollow Shooting Dog Stake.

Because of World War II, it became necessary for a second organization to be founded. This group was called the American Brittany Club. However, it was, and is, the policy of the AKC to recognize only one organization as the official breed club. It was not until July of 1944, after the two clubs had merged under the name The American Brittany Club, that the AKC named the latter as the official parent club.

World War II did a great deal of damage to the Brittany Spaniel in Europe, depleting the breed's gene pool to an alarmingly low level. Brittany fanciers in America rallied to the cause and sent stock to France to help get the breed re-established. In order to assist the effort, the previously barred black color was readmitted in France. It was felt that the gene pool in the US was sufficiently rich, so there was no need to change the standard and allow black coloration.

Meanwhile, a large number of Brittany Spaniels had been imported from France and other parts of Europe since the end of the war. Extensive interbreeding has occurred between the European and American dogs so that today it is impossible to clearly determine a Brittany's actual origin. However, black coloration does remain a disqualification in the AKC standard.

Brittany devotees have always been adamant in protecting the breed's ability to do field work, but they also wanted the breed to receive equal consideration in conformation as a member of the Sporting Group. Ch. Queen of Paradise, owned by Walter S. Oberlin, was the first Brittany to win the Sporting Group at Ravenna, Ohio, in September of 1946 under Judge William L. Kendrick.

Developed around the 1850s in France, the Brittany is the offspring of early land spaniels that were crossed with setters in the Bretagne region of France. It was from the breed's area of development that the Brittany derived its name.

Unlike the rest of the spaniels, the Brittany points to his game rather than flushes it, which is why the Brittany Spaniel in the US officially became the Brittany in September of 1982.

The 1950s were good years for the Brittany, as more and more quality specimens of the breed followed Ch. Queen of Paradise to recognition in Sporting Group competition. In 1957, Ch. Havre Des Bopis Henri broke the Best in Show barrier at the Livonia Kennel Club under Judge Selwyn Harris. Henri was bred, owned, and shown by Paul R. Vollmar.

He remained unique in his achievement until August of 1971, when Ch. Beelflower Dirty Dan, owned and shown by Paul and Linda Mooney, became the breed's second Best in Show winner at Salinas, California under Judge Maxwell Riddle.

SPANIEL OR SETTER?

From its earliest days in America, there were many people who wanted the "Spaniel" removed from the Brittany's name. Their reason was that the Brittany is really a small setter because he points

to his game rather than flushing it like the rest of the spaniels. The argument was waged for many years, but it was not until a meeting of the AKC Board of Directors in April of 1982 that the name change was approved. The Brittany Spaniel officially became the Brittany in September of 1982.

This name change has created a unique situation in the breed. Any French-bred and registered Brittany Spaniel can be imported into the US and registered by the AKC as a Brittany. The dog can be shown and hunted in any AKC events and can compete in obedience trials; however, any Brittany with black in his coat will be disqualified from the conformation ring.

Without a doubt, the dedication of the breeders has enabled the Brittany to surpass others in the field, win in the conformation ring, and excel as a treasured family companion.

Characteristics of the Brittany

Traditionally a hunting dog, the Brittany is very adaptable and fits happily into the role of companion and pet. Because he is relatively small in size, he is easy to keep in either a home or an apartment and fits comfortably in the family car. The Brittany's size is no gauge of his endurance and stamina. He will hunt all day, even for days on end, and will valiantly track down, point, and retrieve grouse, pheasant, woodcock, or quail. Many Brittanys are also adept water dogs, and if given the training and experience, will retrieve waterfowl for the gunner.

Although this seems like a lot of energy wrapped up in a dog weighing a little more than 30 pounds and standing about 19 inches high, he would not be a true Brittany if he were not able to be both rugged in the field and comfortable in the home with his family.

The Brittany has two distinctive characteristics that set him apart from other sporting breeds. Although he is a spaniel, he has an inherent pointing instinct. Unlike the Cocker and English Springer Spaniels that spring or flush their game from cover, the Brittany ranges over the

Whether acting as a hunting companion or loyal family pet, the Brittany has an adaptable personality that allows him to play any role with ease.

Well mannered and sensitive, the Brittany has a natural reserve and responds accordingly to his master's moods.

ground and points to game as the setters do—he is the only spaniel breed known that has this strongly developed instinct. The other distinctive characteristic of the Brittany is his appearance. His ears are set high and held well cocked, and his generally keen and alert look is a very different expression from other spaniels or setters. This intelligent expression is indicative of his character. He has plenty of energy, yet he is neither nervous nor high-strung. He is confident and determined and will not back down from dogs twice his size, but still retains the calm of an understanding companion.

The Brittany has a natural reserve. When it is pronounced, as it may be in some individuals, it might be taken for timidity. However, the average Brittany should not be at all shy; he is just not the kind of dog that climbs in your lap or demands affection. He will show his devotion by lying nearby, watching and responding to your mood. He is sensitive, perhaps even a little standoffish with strangers, and his eyes are only for his family.

Like most dogs of the hunting breeds, the Brittany has quick intelligence, good judgement, athleticism, and the ability to learn. He can be trained for almost any event or competition you may wish him to participate in, and he will gladly return your attention and affection.

Complete with an alert, intelligent expression and an energetic demeanor, the Brittany's distinctive appearance sets him apart from other breeds.

THE GUIDE TO OWNING A BRITTANY

The Official Standard for the Brittany

General Appearance—A compact, closely knit dog of medium size, a leggy dog having the appearance, as well as the agility, of a great ground coverer. Strong, vigorous, energetic and quick of movement. Ruggedness, without clumsiness, is a characteristic of the breed. He can be tailless or has a tail docked to approximately four inches.

Size, Proportion, Substance—*Height*— 17 1/2 to 20 1/2 inches, measured from the ground to the highest point of the shoulders. Any Brittany measuring under 17 1/2 inches or over 20 1/2 inches shall be disqualified from dog show competition. **Weight**—Should weigh between 30 and 40 pounds.

Proportion—So leggy is he that his height at the shoulders is the same as the length of his body.

Body Length—Approximately the same as the height when measured at the shoulders. Body length is measured from

According to the breed standard, the Brittany is a compact, medium-sized dog, with a strength and graceful ruggedness that are characteristic of the breed.

the point of the forecast to the rear of the rump. A long body should be heavily penalized.

Substance—Not too light in bone, yet never heavy-boned and cumbersome.

Head—*Expression*—Alert and eager, but with the soft expression of a bird dog.

Eyes—Well set in head. Well protected from briers by a heavy, expressive eyebrow. A prominent, full or popeye should be heavily penalized. It is a serious fault in a dog that must face briers. Skull well chiseled under the eyes, so that the lower lid is not pulled back to form a pocket or haw that would catch seeds, dirt and weed dust. Preference should be for the darker colored eyes, though lighter shades of amber should not be penalized. Light and

The Brittany is well known for his alert and eager expression, which also carries the soft gaze of a bird dog.

mean-looking eyes should be heavily penalized.

Ears—Set high, above the level of the eyes. Short and triangular, rather than pendulous, reaching about half the length of the muzzle. Should lie flat and close to the head, with the tip rounded very slightly. Ears well covered with dense, but relatively short hair, and with little fringe.

Skull—Medium length, rounded, very slightly wedge-shaped, but evenly made. Width, not quite as wide as the length and never so broad as to appear coarse, or so narrow as to appear racy. Well defined, but gently sloping stop. Median line rather indistinct. The occiput only apparent to the touch. Lateral walls well rounded. The Brittany should never be "apple-headed" and he should never have an indented stop.

Muzzle—Medium length, about two thirds the length of the skull, measuring the muzzle from the tip to the stop, and the skull from the occiput to the stop. Muzzle should taper gradually in both horizontal and vertical dimensions as it approaches the nostrils. Neither a Roman nose nor a dish-face is desirable. Never broad, heavy or snipy.

Nose—Nostrils well open to permit deep breathing of air and adequate scenting. Tight nostrils should be penalized. Never shiny. Color: fawn, tan, shades of brown or deep pink. A black nose is a disqualification. A two-tone or butterfly nose should be penalized.

Lips—Tight, the upper lip overlapping the lower jaw just to cover the lower lip.

Lips dry, so that feathers will not stick. Drooling to be heavily penalized. Flews to be penalized.

Bite—A true scissors bite. Overshot or undershot jaw to be heavily penalized.

Neck, Topline, Body—*Neck*—Medium length. Free from throatiness, though not a serious fault unless accompanied by dewlaps, strong without giving the impression of being overmuscled. Well set into sloping shoulders. Never concave or ewe-necked.

Topline—Slight slope from the highest point of the shoulders to the root of the tail.

Chest—Deep, reaching the level of the elbow. Neither so wide nor so rounded as to disturb the placement of the shoulders and elbows. Ribs well sprung. Adequate heart room provided by depth as well as width. Narrow or slab-sided chests are a fault.

Back—Short and straight. Never hollow, saddle, sway or roach backed. Slight drop from the hips to the root of the tail.

Flanks—Rounded. Fairly full. Not extremely tucked up, or flabby and falling. Loins short and strong. Distance from last rib to upper thigh short, about three to four finger widths. Narrow and weak loins are a fault. In motion, the loin should not sway sideways, giving a zig-zag motion to the back, wasting energy.

Tail—Tailless to approximately four inches, natural or docked. The tail not to be so long as to affect the overall balance of the dog. Set on high, actually an extension of the spine at about the same

The Brittany has high-set ears that lie close to the head and a medium-length muzzle.

level. Any tail substantially more than four inches shall be severely penalized.

Forequarters—*Shoulders*—Shoulder blades should not protrude too much, not too wide apart, with perhaps two thumbs' width between. Sloping and muscular. Blade and upper arm should form nearly a ninety degree angle. Straight shoulders are a fault. At the shoulders the Brittany is slightly higher than at the rump.

Front Legs—Viewed from the front, perpendicular, but not set too wide. Elbows and feet turning neither in nor out. Pasterns slightly sloped. Down in pasterns is a serious fault. Leg bones clean, graceful, but not too fine. Extremely heavy bone is as much a fault as spindly legs. One must look for substance and suppleness. Height at elbows should approximately equal distance from elbow to withers.

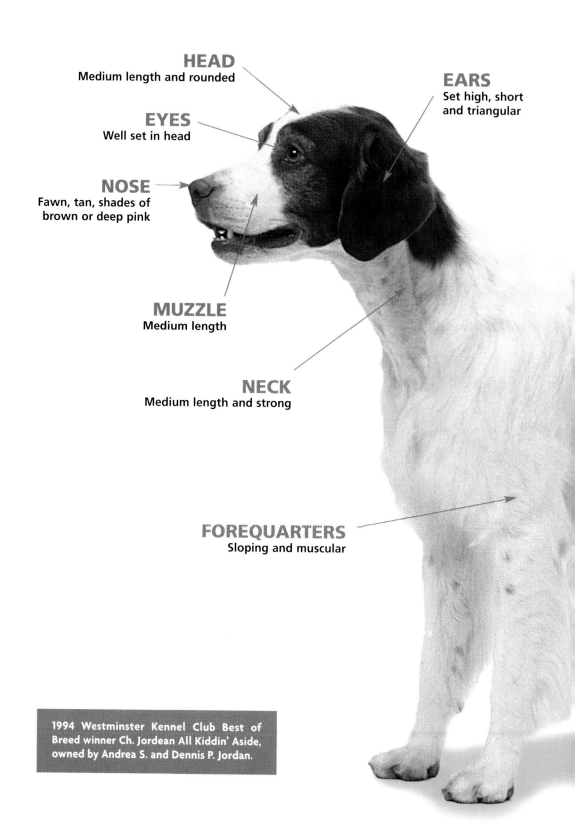

HEAD
Medium length and rounded

EYES
Well set in head

NOSE
Fawn, tan, shades of
brown or deep pink

MUZZLE
Medium length

NECK
Medium length and strong

EARS
Set high, short
and triangular

FOREQUARTERS
Sloping and muscular

1994 Westminster Kennel Club Best of
Breed winner Ch. Jordean All Kiddin' Aside,
owned by Andrea S. and Dennis P. Jordan.

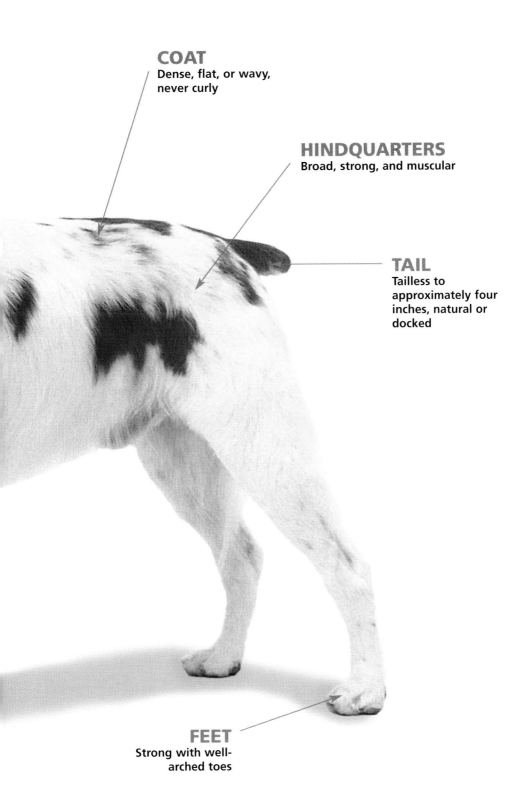

COAT
Dense, flat, or wavy, never curly

HINDQUARTERS
Broad, strong, and muscular

TAIL
Tailless to approximately four inches, natural or docked

FEET
Strong with well-arched toes

Leggy and quick in movement, the Brittany possesses strength and vigor, without appearing clumsy.

Feet—Should be strong, proportionately smaller than the spaniels', with close fitting, well arched toes and thick pads. The Brittany is "not up on his toes." Toes not heavily feathered. Flat feet, splayed feet, paper feet, etc., are to be heavily penalized. An ideal foot is halfway between the hare and the cat foot. Dewclaws may be removed.

Hindquarters—Broad strong and muscular, with powerful thighs and well bent stifles, giving the angulation necessary for powerful drive.

Hind Legs—Stifles well bent. The stifle should not be so angulated as to place the hock joint far out behind the dog. A Brittany should not be condemned for straight stifle until the judge has checked the dog in motion from the side. The stifle joint should not turn out making a cowhock. Thighs well feathered but not profusely, halfway to the hock. Hocks, that is, the back pasterns, should be moderately short, pointing neither in nor out, perpendicular when viewed from the side. They should be firm when shaken by the judge.

Feet—Same as front feet.

Coat—Dense, flat or wavy, never curly. Texture neither wiry nor silky. Ears should carry little fringe. The front and hind legs should have some feathering, but too little is definitely preferable to too much. Dogs with long or profuse feathering or furnishings shall be so severely penalized

The Brittany's coat is either flat or wavy, but never curly. Acceptable coat colors are orange and white or liver and white in either clear or roan patterns.

The Brittany's smooth and efficient gate is an advantage in the field.

as to effectively eliminate them from competition.

Skin—Fine and fairly loose. A loose skin rolls with briers and sticks, thus diminishing punctures or tearing. A skin so loose as to form pouches is undesirable.

Color—Orange and white or liver and white in either clear or roan patterns. Some ticking is desirable. The orange or liver is found in the standard parti-color or piebald patterns. Washed out colors are not desirable. Tri-colors are allowed but not preferred. A tri-color is a liver and white dog with classic orange markings on eyebrows, muzzle and cheeks, inside the ears and under the tail, freckles on the lower legs are orange. Anything exceeding the limits of these markings shall be severely penalized. Black is a disqualification.

Gait—When at a trot the Brittany's hind foot should step into or beyond the print left by the front foot. Clean movement, coming and going, is very important, but most important is side gait, which is smooth, efficient and ground covering.

Temperament—A happy, alert dog, neither mean nor shy.

DISQUALIFICATIONS

Any Brittany measuring under 17 1/2 inches or over 20 1/2 inches.

A black nose.

Black in the coat.

Approved April 10, 1990

Effective May 31, 1990

Selecting Your Brittany

The purchase of any dog is an important step because the well-cared-for Brittany will live with you for many years. Once the prospective Brittany owner decides that he is definitely ready for the responsibilities of dog ownership, he will undoubtedly want to rush out and

Purchasing your Brittany from a reliable, knowledgeable breeder ensures that he is less prone to develop health problems.

purchase a puppy right away. This is not a good idea. It is extremely important that anyone considering taking home a Brittany thoroughly researches the breed. The Brittany is not the breed for everyone. He is a dog that will require lots of time, attention, and training, as well as plenty of outdoor activity. You must be certain that a Brittany will fit in with your family, home environment, and lifestyle.

It is very important that your Brittany be purchased from a breeder who has earned a reputation for consistently producing dogs that are physically healthy and mentally sound. Breeders earn that reputation for quality by selectively breeding their dogs. Selective breeding aims to maintain the virtues of a breed and eliminate genetic weaknesses. The American Kennel Club or the American Brittany Club can assist a prospective dog buyer in finding a responsible breeder of quality stock.

Finding a responsible Brittany breeder may take some time. He or she should have extensive knowledge of the breed, including any genetic problems that may exist.

The responsible Brittany breeder will breed for good temperament far ahead of any other characteristic and will ensure that their puppies are properly socialized. The socialization process should not be overlooked. Proper socialization will help produce a mentally stable dog that will be able to get along with all kinds of people and other animals. A well-socialized Brittany will not show fear, shyness, or aggressiveness. Because Brittany pups need human contact right from the beginning, it is important that the breeder spend a lot of time with each puppy individually to establish the human canine relationship. Ideally, the Brittany should come from working stock, as the dog that demonstrates an ability to retrieve will be a much more intelligent and trainable companion, and will most likely produce offspring with the same qualities.

With any luck, you will be able to find a reputable breeder residing in your area who will not only be able to provide the right Brittany for you, but who will have the parents of the puppy on the premises as well. Meeting the parents of the puppy gives you an opportunity to see firsthand what kind of dogs you puppy comes from. The parents of the puppy should be certified with the Orthopedic Foundation for Animals (OFA) as free of hip dysplasia and the Canine Eye Registration Foundation (CERF) as free of hereditary eye diseases such as cataracts and progressive retinal atrophy. Good breeders are not only willing to have you see the dam (mother) and sire (father) of the litter, but also to inspect the facility in which the dogs are raised. These breeders will also be able to discuss with you any genetic problems that exist in the breed, how they deal with these problems, and how they take measures to safeguard against them.

Be prepared to answer breeders' questions concerning your lifestyle and living conditions. They want to ensure that their puppies go to stable, loving, and permanent homes.

Do not be surprised if a concerned breeder asks lots of questions about you, your family, and the environment in which your Brittany will be raised. Good breeders are just as concerned that their dogs are going to good homes as you, the buyer, are in obtaining a well-adjusted, healthy dog. The breeder will use all the information you give him to match the right puppy with the right home. For example, a quiet, single adult generally needs a puppy with a different personality from the Brittany that is appropriate for a household full of young and energetic children. A person who takes home a Brittany should be able to provide him with the exercise and positive outlets that this breed requires. The time you spend in making the right selection ensures you get the right dog for your lifestyle.

If there are no local breeders in your area, there are legitimate and reliable breeders throughout the country that will appear on the American Brittany Club or national kennel club lists. These established breeders safely ship puppies to different states and even different countries. Always check the references of these breeders and do not hesitate to ask for documentation of their answers. The breeder will undoubtedly have as many questions for you as you will have for him or her. Getting all the information you can to the breeder will ensure that you get the pup with the temperament best suited for you.

Most breeders will not allow their puppies to go to their new homes until after they have been given their first vaccinations—usually at about seven weeks of age. Once weaned, your pup is highly susceptible to many infectious diseases that can be transmitted through people. It is best to make sure your puppy is fully inoculated before he leaves the breeder's residence. You should continue his immunization schedule with your veterinarian.

When arriving at the breeder's home or kennel, the buyer should look for cleanliness in both the dogs and the areas in which the dogs are kept. The cleanliness of the dogs and the condition of the area in which they sleep and play strongly indicate how well the breeder treats the puppies.

A healthy little Brittany puppy should be strong and sturdy to the touch, neither too thin nor obese and bloated. The coat should be shiny and clean, with no sign of dry or flaky skin. The puppy's eyes should be clear, bright, and free of redness or irritation. The inside of the puppy's ears should be pink—discharge or a bad odor could indicate ear mites or infection. A pup that coughs, has diarrhea, or has any eruptions on the skin is usually ill and should not be considered. In fact, if one puppy shows signs of illness, the health of the whole litter must be questioned.

A healthy Brittany puppy should be strong and sturdy with a shiny, clean coat and clear, bright eyes.

When visiting a breeder, make sure that both the dogs and the facilities are clean and well kept.

As you are making a commitment to the puppy for his lifetime, make sure he reacts positively toward you and members of your family. Select the puppy that seems outgoing and ready to trust you. Sit down with the puppies and see which one is interested in playing. If you are looking for strictly a companion pet, pick the puppy that wants to be with you and enjoys your company. Take the puppy you are interested in away from his littermates into another room or another part of the kennel. The smells will remain the same for the puppy, so he should still feel secure and maintain his personality, but it will give you an opportunity to inspect the puppy more closely without distractions. If the puppy ignores you or seems more interested in going back to his littermates, choose another one.

When you purchase your Brittany, remember that the purchase of any

A breeder should supply you with the necessary documents including a pedigree, which helps determine your Brittany's trainability and work ethic.

purebred dog entitles you to three very important documents: a copy of the dog's pedigree, a health record containing an inoculation schedule, and the dog's registration certificate.

PEDIGREE
The breeder must supply you with a copy of your Brittany's pedigree, a document that authenticates your puppy's ancestors back to at least the third generation. All purebred dogs have a pedigree. The pedigree does not imply that a dog is of show quality, but is simply a chronological list of ancestors. The pedigree can be helpful in determining if your Brittany's relatives have any titles in obedience or field trials, which can indicate the trainability and work ethic of the pup's parents and grandparents.

HEALTH RECORD
The Brittany breeder that you buy your puppy from should have initiated the necessary inoculation series for the litter by the time they are eight weeks of age. These inoculations protect the puppies against hepatitis, leptospirosis, distemper, and canine parvovirus. In most cases, rabies inoculations are not given until a puppy is four months of age or older.

These inoculations are given as a series, and it is very important that your Brittany puppy receives the full set in order for them to be effective. The veterinarian you choose will then be able to continue on an appropriate inoculation schedule.

REGISTRATION CERTIFICATE
A country's governing kennel club issues this certificate. When you transfer the ownership of your Brittany from the breeder's name to your own name, the transaction is entered on this certificate. Once this is mailed to the kennel club, it is permanently recorded in their files. You will need to produce this document if you decide to show your Brittany.

DIET
Most breeders will give the new owner a written record that details the amount and kind of food a puppy has been eating. Follow these recommendations exactly at least for the first month or two after the puppy comes to live with you. The instructions should indicate the number of times a day your puppy has been fed and the kind of vitamin supplementation

he has been receiving, if any. If you follow the breeder's instructions it will greatly reduce the chance of your Brittany puppy suffering from an upset stomach and diarrhea.

The breeder's diet sheet should project the increases and changes in food that will be necessary as your puppy grows from week to week. If the breeder does not provide you with this information, ask your veterinarian for suggestions. If and when you decide to change the type or brand of dog food you are giving your Brittany, do so gradually, mixing the old food with the new until the substitution is completed.

HEALTH GUARANTEE

Any reputable breeder will be more than willing to supply a written agreement that the puppy you choose to take home must be able to pass a veterinarian's

Arrange to take your Brittany to the vet within 24 hours after picking him up from the breeder.

Exposing your Brittany puppy to as many new situations as possible will sharpen his socialization skills as well as provide him with stimulating activities.

examination. Furthermore, the puppy should be guaranteed against the development of any hereditary problems. You should choose a veterinarian before deciding on your Brittany and arrange an appointment with him right after you have picked up your puppy from the breeder and before you take the puppy home. If this is not possible, you should not delay this procedure any longer than 24 hours after the puppy leaves the breeder's residence.

SOCIALIZATION

A Brittany's temperament is both hereditary and learned. A Brittany pup can inherit a bad temperament from one or both of his parents and will definitely not make a good pet or working dog. Bad temperament can also be caused by a lack of socialization or mistreatment. The first step in getting a stable and well-adjusted companion is obtaining a happy puppy from a breeder who is determined to produce good temperaments and has taken all the necessary steps to provide early socialization. Your puppy should stay with his dam and littermates until at least seven weeks of age, because the interaction with them will help your Brittany get along with other dogs later in life.

Once you bring your Brittany puppy home, it is necessary to continue the socialization started by the breeder. You should introduce your Brittany puppy to everyone, especially children. If you have young ones in your family, teach them to treat the puppy with respect. If you do not have children, find some gentle children to play with your puppy. Energetic children make wonderful playmates for the energetic Brittany—and vice versa.

Take the puppy to as many different environments as you can—the beach, the park, the store, and the car. Expose him to different noises and situations, such as busy streets or crowded pet stores, always on lead, of course. Introduce him to other well-socialized dogs. All Brittanys must learn to get along with other dogs as well as with humans. Find a "puppy kindergarten" class in your area and attend regularly. Not only is it a great place to socialize your dog, it is also the first step in training the new addition to your family.

Feeding Your Brittany

Good nutrition is a necessary requirement in your Brittany's life. Providing your dog with the proper diet is one of the most important aspects of caring for him. By carefully researching which diet is the best one, you can ensure his good health, which will affect all other parts of your life together.

DOG FOODS

If you take a trip to your local pet emporium or supermarket, you cannot help but notice that there is an overwhelming selection of dog foods available. It can be confusing, to say the least, and it makes it hard to choose which brand is best for your Brittany. There are certain things you should know about commercial dog food that will help you make the right decision. The more you educate yourself about what his nutritional needs are, the easier the decision will be.

In order to stay healthy, there are six essential nutrients that all dogs in every stage of life need in varied amounts: protein, fat, carbohydrates, vitamins, minerals, and water.

Protein

Protein can be burned as calories and stored as fat. It helps with muscle growth, tissue repair, blood clotting, and immunity functions. Good sources of protein are meat, fish, poultry, milk, cheese, yogurt, fishmeal, and eggs.

Fat

Fat supplies the energy needed for the absorption of certain vitamins, provides insulation from cold, and makes food tastier. Fat can be found in meat and meat by-products and vegetable oils, such as safflower, olive, corn, or soybean.

Carbohydrates

Carbohydrates provide energy and keep intestines functioning smoothly. Complex carbohydrates are fiber and sugar and can

In addition to exercise and care, dogs need the proper nutrition. Make sure that you choose foods containing the essential ingredients that your Brittany needs to maintain good health.

be found in corn, oats, wheat, rice, and barley.

Vitamins

Vitamins are divided into two groups—water-soluble and fat-soluble. Different vitamins have different functions: Vitamin A protects skin and promotes bone growth; Vitamin B aids in metabolism; Vitamin D aids in bone growth and increases calcium absorption; and Vitamin K helps with blood clotting. Good sources of vitamins are fruit, vegetables, cereals, and the liver of most animals.

Minerals

Minerals provide strength to bone and ensure proper bone formation, maintain fluid balance and normal muscle and nerve function, transport oxygen to the blood, and produce hormones. Examples of minerals are calcium, phosphorus, copper, iron, magnesium, selenium, potassium, zinc, and sodium.

Water

The most important of all nutrients, water makes up over 60 percent of a dog. Water intake can come directly through drinking or can be released when food is oxidized. If your dog's diet is lacking in water, dehydration can occur, which can lead to serious breakdown of organs or even death. All dogs must maintain a water balance, which means that their total intake of water should be in balance with the total output. Make sure that your puppy has access to cool, clean water at all times.

TYPES OF DOG FOOD

First, you should pick a dog food that is specially formulated for active dogs. This will ensure that your Brittany is getting the proper nutrition for growth and digestion for his undeveloped systems. There are three types of dog food available on the market today, and all of them have good and bad points. You must choose the type that best fits you and your puppy's needs.

Dry Food

The good thing about dry food is that it is the least expensive, can conveniently be left in bowl for longer periods of time, and helps control tartar. However, it is the least appealing to dogs.

Canned food

Canned food is the most appealing to dogs, but it spoils quickly, is the most expensive, and requires more to be fed because the energy content is relatively low, especially for large or active breeds.

Semi-Moist

Semi-moist food will not spoil at room temperature and comes in prepackaged servings, but it also contains large amounts of sugar and preservatives in order to remain fresh without refrigeration.

READING LABELS

There are two agencies that work together in regulating pet food labels. The first agency, the Association of American Feed Control Officials (AAFCO), is a non-governmental agency made up of state and federal officials from around the United States. They establish pet food regulations that cover areas like guaranteed analysis, nutritional adequacy statements, and feeding directions. Each state decides whether or not to enforce AAFCO's regulations. Most do; however, some do not.

The second agency, the Food and Drug Administration Center for Veterinary Medicine, establishes and enforces standards for all animal feed. This federal agency oversees aspects of labeling that covers proper identification of products, net quantity statements, and the list of ingredients.

Learn how to read dog food labels, especially when you consider how many brands are out there. Slight changes in wording can make the difference between a quality dog food and one that may not appear to be what it seems.

PRODUCT NAME

You may think the name of your dog food is just a name, but in most cases, it can make a big difference. Specific words used in the name can indicate what is in the food and what is not. For example, a brand name like "Beef Dog Food" must contain at least 95 percent beef, but if it is called "Beef *Formula* for Dogs," it is required to contain a minimum of only 25 percent beef. Other words like dinner, platter, nuggets, or entrée fall under this 25 percent minimum requirement.

Another word to watch for is "with." A dog food called "Dog Food *with* Beef" only has to contain a minimum of 3

Because of the Brittany's energetic nature, it's best to choose a dog food specially formulated for active dogs.

Your Brittany should have a healthy diet that includes the proper amount of fats, proteins, and carbohydrates.

percent beef. The word "with" was originally supposed to highlight extra ingredients, but recent amendments to AAFCO regulations now allow the word to be used in the product's name. Also, the word "flavored" can be deceiving, because it means that only a sufficient amount of flavoring needs to be added for it to be detectable. Therefore "Beef *Flavored* Dog Food" may not include any beef at all and may only be flavored with very small amounts of beef by-products.

INGREDIENT LIST

Each ingredient contained in the dog food will be listed in descending order according to weight. However, the quality of each ingredient is not required to be listed. For best results, look for animal-based proteins to be high up on the list, such as beef, beef by-products, chicken, chicken by-products, lamb, lamb meal, fish meal, and egg. However, use caution and read carefully, because some manufacturers will manipulate the weight of products in order to place it higher or lower on the list. For example, they may divide the grains into different categories, like wheat flour and whole ground wheat, in order to lower the weight and make it seem less prominent on the ingredient list.

You may be wondering what exactly are meat by-products and meal, anyway. Actual "meat" is considered to be the clean flesh of a slaughtered mammal and is limited to the part of the striate muscle that is skeletal or found in the tongue, diaphragm, heart, or esophagus. Meat by-products are the non-rendered lean parts other than the meat, which includes, but is not limited to, the lungs, spleen, kidney, bone, blood, stomach, intestines, necks, feet, and undeveloped eggs. Meat and bone meal is the rendered product or mammal tissue, which includes bone, hair hood, horn, hide trimming, manure, and stomach. As you can see, the ingredients in dog food can vary widely, so be informed about what your puppy is actually eating.

GUARANTEED ANALYSIS

The guaranteed analysis states the minimum amounts of crude protein and crude fat, as well as the maximum amount percentage of moisture (water) and crude fiber. The word "crude" refers to the method of testing the product, not the quality of the nutrient. Sometimes manufactures will list other nutrients like ash or calcium, although they are not required to do so.

NUTRITIONAL ADEQUACY STATEMENT

The nutritional adequacy statement is important when looking for a dog food for puppies because it states what life stage the product is formulated for, such as growth, reproduction, maintenance, senior, or all life stages. For developing puppies, look for the product that is specially formulated for growth. It should also tell you whether the product is "complete and balanced" or "complementary." Complete and balanced means that it contains all the ingredients your dog will need on a daily basis and that it can be served by itself.

Complementary means that it is not intended to be used alone and must be added to another product to create a complete meal.

NET QUANTITY STATEMENT

The net quality statement shows the weight of the food in the bag or can in pounds and ounces as well as metric weight. Be careful, because some companies use 30-pound bags and then only put 25 pounds of food inside.

FEEDING INSTRUCTIONS

The feeding instructions on the dog food label are only suggestions; some dogs will eat more, some will eat less. Also, they are the amounts needed for the entire day, so you can divide it up the best way for you and your puppy. If you are not sure how much to feed, start off

The best way to determine if your puppy's diet is sufficient is by checking his bone and muscle development, his level of activity, and his weight.

Your breeder should supply you with a diet sheet. Maintain this original diet and make any changes gradually to avoid stomach upsets.

with the suggested amount and increase or decrease as necessary.

Although dog food labels tell you a lot about a product, there is a lot that they don't tell you. For example, some wording used on labels can be misleading. Foods that use the words "gourmet" or "premium" are not required to contain any higher quality ingredients than any other product. Products that claim to be "all-natural" are not required to be. Some might think that this means the food is minimally processed or contains no artificial ingredients, but this is not necessarily true. In fact, all dog foods must contain some chemically synthesized ingredients in order to be deemed complete and balanced.

HOMEMADE DIETS

There seems to be a debate about whether a homemade diet is better for your dog than manufactured dog food. The downside to feeding a homemade diet is that you need to be very careful to ensure that you are providing your puppy with all of the necessary nutrients. It also takes a lot of time, effort, and energy to cook a proper diet for your dog on a daily basis.

Those that are in favor of a homemade diet believe that commercial dog foods contain contaminated and unhealthy ingredients and feel that it is worth the effort to give their puppy a home-cooked meal. If you have the time and money, and believe that it is important to feed your puppy a homemade diet, consult your veterinarian who can give you a reputable and nutritionally balanced recipe. Although millions of dogs exist and stay healthy on commercially prepared dog food, the ultimate decision is yours.

Now that you have learned all you can about dog food and feeding options, you can make an informed choice about what to buy for your puppy.

FEEDING YOUR BRITTANY PUPPY

If you are lucky, the breeder from whom you obtained your puppy will have given you a diet sheet which will help you immensely with your feeding chores. A diet sheet will typically tell you the type of food your puppy has been eating, when he eats, and how to increase his food intake as he ages. Some breeders will even include enough food to get you through a day or two. If possible, follow this original feeding schedule as closely as possible, and use the same brand of puppy food for the first few months. This will help avoid any stomach upsets or diarrhea. If you would like to change the brand of food your puppy is eating, do so gradually, slowly mixing the old food with the new food over a period of time until the old food is totally replaced.

If no diet sheet was provided for you, you will have to use the information available about dog food and choose one that is specially formulated for puppies. It should indicate that it is a growth formula as well. If you are undecided about which brand to choose, consult your veterinarian.

How will you know if you have made the right choice? First, take a look at your puppy's stool. It should be small and firm, not too loose or too dry. A large amount of

How often you feed your Brittany depends on his age. For example, 8- to 16-week-old puppies need 3 or 4 meals a day; older dogs only require 2 meals a day.

Your Brittany will let you know if he is getting the right amount of food. For example, if he quickly devours his meal, you may have to increase the quantity of food.

stool means the food is not being digested. Although it may take a few months to notice, a puppy eating a nutritious diet will have all the signs of good health, including a glossy coat, high energy, and bright eyes.

WHEN TO FEED

Start off with light, frequent meals because your puppy's stomach is so small. If the breeder has included a feeding schedule with your diet sheet, follow that as closely as possible and make increases or decreases as recommended. If no feeding schedule accompanied your puppy, set one up right away.

A four-month old (or younger) puppy should be fed four times a day. At four to six months of age, you can reduce the feedings to three, and after six months, you can start feeding once or twice a day,

depending on your schedule. You should always feed him at the same time of day starting out with breakfast, lunch, mid-afternoon snack, and dinner, which should be served an hour before bedtime. Take your puppy outside to go potty as soon as he is finished with his meal.

Some people recommend "free feeding" your dog, which means leaving food out for him to nibble on all day. This makes it harder to judge exactly how much the dog has eaten and makes it harder to predict when the dog needs to go outside to eliminate. It also could lead to overeating, because many Brittanys will eat out of boredom. It is best to put the food down for your puppy for a limited time and then take the food away when the time is up. Your puppy will adjust quickly to the schedule, and you'll have more control over the amount consumed.

HOW MUCH TO FEED

If you don't know the puppy's prior feeding schedule, you will have to figure out how much to feed him. Start off by following the directions on the dog food label and increase or decrease the amount as needed. Give the recommended amount for your puppy's age and take it away after a period of time. If your puppy eats the food quickly and leaves nothing, you need to increase the amount. If there is leftover food, you may have to decrease the amount or feed smaller meals more frequently.

TREATS

Treats are a great way to encourage and reward your Brittany for doing something well. There are plenty of treats available today that are not only tasty but also nutritious. Hard biscuits can help keep his teeth clean. Remember to consider treats as part of your dog's total food intake. Limit the amount of treats you give your puppy, and be sure to feed him only healthy snacks. Avoid giving him table scraps, as they usually just add to his caloric intake. Obesity is a very serious health problem in dogs, so be sure to start your puppy off eating right.

BONES

Bones can help your puppy with his overwhelming need to chew. They keep his teeth clean and keep him from becoming bored. Make sure you give your dog safe bones and toys made especially for dogs, those that will not splinter or break into tiny pieces. Pieces can be swallowed and become stuck in your puppy's intestinal tract or cause him to choke. There are plenty of manufacturers that make safe, chewable, and edible dog bones, so give your Brittany something fun and safe as a special treat.

SUPPLEMENTS

Healthy puppies that are fed a balanced diet will not need supplementation. In fact, some veterinarians believe that supplementing your puppy's diet with extra vitamins and minerals can aggravate conditions like hip dysplasia and hereditary skin problems. The only time you should give your puppy any kind of supplements is under the direction of your veterinarian and even then you should never exceed the prescribed amount.

Make sure that you give your Brittany safe chew toys that are made especially for dogs.

Grooming Your Brittany

The Brittany is a breed that requires very minimal grooming to look his best. However, your dog will rely on regular grooming to keep him healthy. Grooming is also important because it gives you a

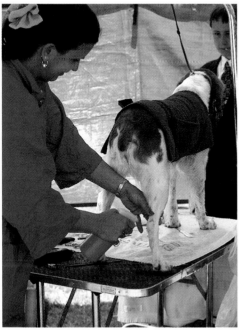

If you accustom your Brittany to grooming at any early age, he will come to enjoy the time that you spend together.

chance to inspect your dog and catch any skin or health problems before they start. If you work with your Brittany in the field, regular grooming is very important, especially after spending time outdoors. Be sure to check your dog's coat thoroughly for burrs, grasses, thorns, or anything he may have picked up while in the field.

Puppyhood is the best time to start grooming procedures. Your dog will become easily used to the grooming routine and soon come to expect it as part of everyday life. It is best to invest in a good grooming table if you plan to show your Brittany. While he is getting beautiful, your dog's leash can be attached to the grooming arm on the table, which will help keep him secure. Most tables have non-skid pads on the surface to keep him from sliding around. A grooming table will save your back as well, because it can be adjusted to your

A Brittany does not require extensive grooming, but a weekly brushing will keep his coat looking healthy and clean.

height and prevent you from having to bend over or kneel down.

Introduce your puppy to the grooming table slowly. Place the pup up there a few times without doing anything to him and give him a treat when you let him down. After you do this a few times, your puppy should eagerly get up on the grooming table. Then you can start lightly brushing him and running any appliances, like hair dryers or clippers, before actually doing any major grooming. When the dog seems totally comfortable, you can start grooming him on a regular basis. This gradual introduction will ensure that your puppy grows to enjoy his grooming time with you.

Once your puppy is accustomed to being touched, patted, and fussed over, you can begin to start a grooming routine that will keep him looking clean and healthy.

BRUSHING

Brushing your Brittany on a daily basis will go a long way to keeping him looking good. Daily brushing will reduce shedding, keep mats to a minimum, and allow you to inspect the coat for any foreign debris or skin problems. It also stimulates your dog's skin and spreads the coat's natural oils, which help keep a coat shiny and the skin healthy. Brushing on a routine basis means your dog will need to be bathed less often, because most of the dirt and debris in his coat will be removed regularly.

Most dogs will thoroughly enjoy the time spent getting pampered by you every day. What puppy can resist lounging on his

Most Brittanys do not need to be bathed often. However, if your puppy has rolled in something smelly or dirty, he will require a bath.

owner's lap while being brushed—it's a canine paradise!

BATHING

Most Brittanys will require a bath only occasionally. Healthy dogs are pretty good at keeping themselves clean, and regular brushing should keep your puppy's coat in good shape. In fact, over-bathing your dog can cause dry skin and irritation, which can cause excess scratching or infections. But every puppy, at some time or another, will roll in something particularly smelly or dirty and require a bath. When you do give your puppy a bath, steps should be taken to make it as painless as possible.

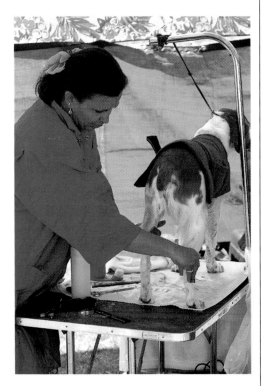

Make grooming time as pleasant as possible for your Brittany by being gentle and rewarding him for good behavior.

THE HUNTING OR UTILITY CLIP

Trimming a Brittany for hunting ahead of time will save you work afterward. The grooming method can be modified to accommodate the situation, so consider the type of terrain you and your dog will cover when you go out in the field.

Begin by lifting the ear and, using scissors, trimming the excess hair on the upper cheek and under the ear. This is one of the worst places for hiding burrs, stickers, and other debris.

Next, hold the ear out and away from the head, cutting off all the hair that is longer than the ear. The hair in the armpits, where the legs join the body, should also be trimmed; however, do not remove all the hair on the belly or it may become scratched or sore in the field.

Feet should be checked before and after field work. Excess hair should be removed from between the toes. Inspect your dog's feet after each outing and check that there are no splinters, burrs, thorns, seeds, or other sharp objects in the pads or between the toes. If you find anything, remove it gently with a pair of tweezers. Some owners prefer to trim the "flag" on the Brittany's tail, but some do not. Trimming his coat will ensure that your Brittany will be better protected— now your Brittany is ready to go to work!

TOENAIL AND FOOT CARE

Your Brittany's feet really take a beating. They endure the pounding of all that energy and traverse the terrain of every place he explores—over rocks, cement, wood, snow, or grass, your pup's feet get there first and suffer the hardest.

It is important to take good care of your dog's paws. Always examine your Brittany's feet as part of his daily grooming. Also watch for soreness or blisters. If your puppy shows any signs of soreness or favors a leg when he walks, take him to the veterinarian immediately.

Nail trimming is something that your dog should get used to in puppyhood. The earlier your Brittany gets used to nail trimming, the easier your life will be at grooming time. Nail trimming is not only for appearances, but is necessary for your puppy's health and comfort. It can be very difficult to get your puppy to sit still for this, which is why it is easier to start while the dog is young. Also, if your puppy has a scary or painful experience, you may not get a second chance, so try to make this procedure as comfortable and routine as possible.

Trimming your puppy's nails is not as hard as it may seem. The easiest way to do it is with a pair of canine nail clippers. You can also use an electric nail grinder, if you find this method easier. Take care to avoid the quick, which is the area of the nail that contains nerves and blood vessels. If you accidentally cut the quick, it will bleed and be painful to your dog.

The Brittany has clear or white nails, so it is fairly easy to see the quick, which looks like a pink line that extends from the base of the nail toward the tip. The best way to trim your puppy's nails is to be conservative and only snip a tiny amount

Although nail trimming may be somewhat uncomfortable for your dog, it is necessary for his health and comfort. It also adds to a clean and neat appearance.

at a time. Once you do it, it is easy to repeat the procedure for each nail, using the previous one as a model. If you do cut the quick, have a styptic pencil or powder on hand to curb the bleeding.

If it makes you too nervous to trim your Brittany's nails *don't ignore the task*. Go to an experienced groomer and let her do it for you. But if you start now and add it to your weekly schedule, you and your puppy will be nail-trimming experts in no time.

EAR CARE

Do not neglect your Brittany's ears when you groom him. Ear infections can be caused by excessive dirt, moisture, and bacteria in the ear canal. Dogs with long, floppy ears, like the Brittany, are especially prone to ear problems because their ear shape prevents good air circulation. Also, dogs that often swim in natural water like lakes or rivers can get bacteria caught in their ear, causing an infection.

When taking care of your Brittany's ears, the first thing you should do is pluck or trim out (with blunt-nosed scissors) the excess hair. To keep them clean, use a cotton ball or washcloth dampened with commercial ear cleaner or mineral oil and wipe the inside of the earflap. If your dog's ear is sore, has excess wax, or has a bad smell, he probably has an ear infection and needs to see the veterinarian immediately.

EYE CARE

It is fairly easy to keep your puppy's eyes clear, sparkling, and bright. First, make sure that you keep all debris, including hair, out of his eyes. Wipe your dog's eyes on a regular basis with a cotton ball or washcloth dipped in warm water. If your puppy's eyes appear red, cloudy, swollen, or have excess tearing, contact your veterinarian.

DENTAL CARE

Puppies need to chew. Chewing is an essential part of their physical and mental development, so you need to take good care of their teeth from the very beginning.

If you do not brush your Brittany's teeth on a regular basis, plaque builds up on the teeth and under the gums. If this plaque is not removed, periodontal disease, which is a bacterial infection, can occur. If left untreated, the bacteria can enter the bloodstream and spread to your puppy's vital organs. Problems such as mouth abscesses and tooth loss can develop as well. Dogs that don't receive good dental care can suffer from really bad breath, a feature that does not endear them to humans.

It is much easier to brush your puppy's

Breeds with long, floppy ears, like the Brittany, are prone to ear problems. It's important that your Brittany's ears remain free from debris.

It's a good idea to let your Brittany get used to having your fingers in his mouth before you begin a brushing routine.

teeth than you may think, as long as you have the right supplies. You should purchase a dog toothbrush or a finger toothbrush (a rubber cap that fits over your index finger) and toothpaste made for dogs. Never use human toothpaste when brushing your puppy's teeth. Dogs will not spit out the toothpaste, which can cause stomach upset and digestive problems. Also, the minty taste that humans enjoy probably will not be as appealing to your puppy as it is to you. Canine toothpaste come in "doggy-friendly" flavors, such as beef and poultry, and are edible.

Start by getting your puppy used to having your fingers in his mouth. When you are performing the daily once-over, be sure to look in your dog's mouth, lifting the dewflaps to expose the gums. Touch the teeth. Soon this will become just another part of your grooming routine. Once he is used to this procedure, put some doggy-flavored toothpaste on the toothbrush and gently rub a few teeth at a time. Be sure to brush the teeth at the gum line.

Use a circular motion when brushing and slowly make your way around your dog's upper teeth. Make sure to get the teeth in the back of the mouth, because these teeth are the ones most prone to periodontal disease. When you are finished with the top, do the bottom in the same manner.

Daily brushing would be ideal, but try to do it at least four times a week. This will keep your Brittany's teeth healthy for a long time.

Training Your Brittany

When you added a Brittany to your family, you probably wanted a companion and a friend. You may have wanted a dog to go for walks, take jogs, or play with your children. Perhaps you wanted to get involved in hunting and field events. To do any of these things, your puppy will need training.

Whether you intend for your Brittany to be a hunting companion or an exercise companion, he will need the proper training.

If you accustom your Brittany to a crate at an early age, he will come to think of it as his home away from home.

Crate training is the easiest and quickest way to housetrain your Brittany.

Good basic training will transform your jumpy, squirmy, wiggly little puppy into a well-mannered Brittany that is a joy to be around. A trained puppy won't jump up on people, dash out the open door, or raid the trash can. He will be able to be all you want him to be. Your puppy needs to have someone tell him what to do. Your Brittany has the right to be trained—it is unfair to leave him to figure out the human world on his own, and he won't be able to do it.

You, too, will benefit from training, because you will learn how to motivate your dog, how to prevent problem behavior, and how to correct mistakes that do happen. Puppy training entails much more than learning the traditional sit, down, stay, and come commands—it means that you will be teaching your puppy to live in your house. You can set some rules and expect him to follow them.

HOUSEHOLD RULES

Start teaching your puppy the household rules as soon as possible—preferably as soon as you get him home. Your eight- to ten-week-old puppy is not too young to learn what you expect of him. When you teach him these rules from the start, you can prevent bad habits from forming.

When deciding what rules you want him to follow, picture your puppy as the adult dog you want him to be. It may be cute to let your little Brittany sleep on your bed every night, but are you going to want a 30-pound bedmate a year from now? Take a practical look at your puppy and your environment and decide what behavior you can or cannot live with. It is important to make these decisions early in your dog's life, because what he learns as a puppy will remain with the adult dog.

HOUSETRAINING

One of the first things that you will undertake will be housetraining your Brittany. You are teaching your dog that he has a specific place that he should eliminate, preferably outside. Your best bet is to start housetraining him as soon as possible. However, you need to remember that puppies between the ages of 8 to 16 weeks do not have control of their bladders or bowels. They are not able to "hold it" until they get a little older, which means that in the beginning, housetraining will take vigilance on your part. You will have to watch very carefully for signs that your puppy needs to eliminate. He will usually have to go to the bathroom after eating, drinking, sleeping, and playing. Most puppies will also give off signals, like circling or sniffing the floor. These behaviors are a sure sign that your puppy needs to go outside. When you see him display this behavior, don't hesitate. Carry your pup outside to the spot where you want him to eliminate. Praise your dog for eliminating in the proper spot.

CRATE TRAINING

With the help of a regular schedule, you will be able to predict the times that your puppy will need to potty. The most useful thing that you can buy for your puppy to help facilitate this process is a crate. Training your puppy to use a crate is the quickest and easiest way to housetrain him. Remember that your Brittany will be developing habits throughout his training that will last him his lifetime—make sure you teach the right ones.

By about five weeks of age, most puppies are starting to move away from their mom and littermates to relieve themselves. This instinct to keep the bed clean is the basis of crate training. Crates work well because puppies do not want to soil where they eat and sleep. They also like to curl up in small dark places that offer them protection on three sides, because it makes them feel more secure. When you provide your puppy with a crate, you are giving him his very own "den"—to your puppy's inner wolf, it is home sweet home. Pups will do their best to eliminate away from their den, and later, away from your house.

Being confined in the crate will help a puppy develop better bowel and bladder control. When confined for gradually extended periods of time, the dog will learn to avoid soiling his bed. It is your responsibility to give your dog plenty of time outside the crate and the house, or the training process will not be successful.

Sometimes puppies really just need to get away from it all. The hustle and bustle of a busy household can be overwhelming

Like humans, canines need private time to relax and wind down. The crate offers your Brittany refuge if he feels overwhelmed.

Be careful never to use the crate as punishment. Try to make your puppy's experiences with the crate positive and enjoyable.

Choosing a Crate

There are two types of crates to choose from—the plastic or fiberglass airline-type crates with enclosed sides and the open metal wire crates. Consider what you will be using the crate for and pick the best one. The plastic crates are good to use for traveling, especially by air, and some dogs feel more secure in an enclosed space. The wire crates provide more ventilation in hotter weather and more room to move around.

A crate is an expensive item, and you will want it to last, so buy a crate that will fit your dog's adult size. An adult dog should be able to stand up, turn around, and stretch out in the crate comfortably. However, you don't want your little puppy to have too much room to roam around in, either. This might become a problem, because he may decide to eliminate in one corner of his big, roomy crate and sleep in the other. The best thing to do is to block off a portion of the crate and make it progressively larger as your dog matures and grows.

Introducing the Crate

Introduce your puppy to the crate very gradually. You want the puppy to feel like this is a pleasant place to be. Begin by opening the door and throwing one of your puppy's favorite treats inside. You may want to teach him a command, like "bedtime" or "crate" when the pup goes into the crate. Let your dog investigate the crate and come and go freely. Don't forget lots of praise. Next, offer a meal in the crate. Put the food dish inside and once inside, close the door

at times. There are times when your puppy will get overstimulated and need to take a "time out" to calm down (especially if you have rambunctious kids around). A crate is great for all of these times. The crate can be used as your puppy's place of refuge. If he's tired, hurt, or sick, he can go back to his crate to sleep or hide. If he's overstimulated or excited, he can be put in his crate to calm down. If you are doing work around the house that doesn't allow you to watch over him, you can put him into his crate until you are done painting the bathroom or the workmen have left. In short, crates are lifesavers for puppy owners. Eventually, the puppy will think that it is pretty cool, too.

behind him. Open the door when he's done eating. Keep this up until your puppy eats all his meals in the crate.

Soon your puppy will become accustomed to going in and out of the crate for treats and meals. If you do not wish to continue feeding him in his crate, you can start feeding elsewhere, but continue offering a treat for going into the crate. Start closing the door and leaving your puppy inside for a few minutes at a time. Gradually increase the amount of time your puppy spends in the crate. Always make sure that you offer him a treat and praise for going in. It is also a good idea to keep a few favorite toys inside the crate as well.

Crate Don'ts

• Don't let your puppy out of the crate when he cries or scratches at the door. If you do, your dog will think that complaining will bring release every time. The best thing to do for a temper tantrum is to ignore the pup. Only open the door when the dog is quiet and has calmed down.

• Don't use the crate as punishment. If you use the crate when he does something bad, your dog will think of the crate as a bad place. Even if you want to get the pup out of the way, make sure that you offer him lots of praise for going into the crate and give a treat or toy too.

Crate Location

During the day, keep your puppy's crate in a location that allows him easy access and permits him to be part of the family. The laundry room or backyard will make a dog feel isolated and unhappy, especially if he can hear people walking around. Place it anywhere the family usually congregates—the kitchen or family room is often the best place.

At night, especially when your puppy is still getting used to the crate, the ideal place for it is in your bedroom, near your bed. Having you nearby will create a feeling of security and be easier for you as well. If the pup needs to go outside during the night, you can let him out before he has an accident. Your dog will also be comforted by the smell, sight, and sound of you and will be less likely to feel frightened.

Teaching your Brittany good manners and obedience skills will ensure that he becomes a good canine citizen and a treasured member of the family.

OUTSIDE SCHEDULE

As was mentioned before, puppies need time to develop bowel and bladder control. The best way to most accurately predict when your Brittany needs to eliminate is to establish a routine that works well for both of you. If you make a daily schedule of eating, drinking, and outside time, you will notice your puppy's progress.

Every person and family will have a different routine—there is no one right schedule for everyone. Just make sure that you arrange times and duties that everyone can stick with. The schedule you set will have to work with your normal routine and lifestyle. Your first priority in the morning will be to get the puppy outdoors. Just how early this will take

An outdoor exercise pen gives your energetic Brittany the chance to exercise while keeping him safely confined.

place will depend much more on your puppy than on you. Once your puppy comes to expect a morning walk, there will be no doubt in your mind when he needs to go out. You will also learn very quickly how to tell a puppy's "emergency" signals. Do not test the young puppy's ability for self-control. A vocal demand to be let out is confirmation that the housetraining lesson is learned.

It is also important to limit your puppy's freedom inside the house and keep a careful eye on him at all times. Many puppies won't take the time to go outside to relieve themselves because they are afraid that they will miss something; after all, everything exciting happens in the house. That's where all the family members usually are. Unfortunately, you may find your puppy sneaking off somewhere—behind the sofa or to another room—to relieve himself. By limiting the puppy's freedom, you can prevent some of these mistakes. Close bedroom doors and put baby gates across hallways. If you can't supervise him, put the dog in the crate or outside in a secure area.

ACCIDENTS WILL HAPPEN

When housetraining your dog, remember, that if the puppy has an accident in the house, it is not his fault, it's yours. It means that the puppy was not supervised well enough or wasn't taken outside in time.

If you catch your dog in the act, don't yell or scold him. Simply say "No!" loudly, which should startle and stop him. Pick your pup up and go outside to continue in the regular relief area. Praise your puppy for finishing outside. If you scold or punish him, you are teaching him that you think going potty is wrong. Your dog will become sneaky about it, and you will find puddles and piles in strange places. Don't concentrate on correction; emphasize the praise for going potty in the right place.

If you find a little surprise left for you, do not yell at your puppy for it and never rub his nose in it. Your puppy will have no idea what you are talking about, and you'll only make him scared of you. Simply clean it up and be sure to keep a closer eye on him next time.

Housetraining is one of the most important gifts that you can give your dog. It allows him to live as one of the family. Every puppy will make mistakes, especially in the beginning. Do not worry—with the proper training and lots of patience, every dog can be housetrained.

BASIC TRAINING

Collar and Leash Training

Training a puppy to a collar and leash is very easy and something you can start doing at home without assistance. Place a soft nylon collar on the puppy. The pup will initially try to bite at it, but will soon forget it's there, more so if you play with him. Some people leave their dog's collar on all of the time: others put it on only when they are taking the dog out. If it is to be left on, purchase a narrow or round one so it does not mark the fur or become snagged on furniture.

Training your Brittany to walk on a leash will give you the chance to enjoy quality time outside together. Be sure to end each lesson with plenty of praise.

Once the puppy ignores his collar, you can attach the leash to it and let him pull it behind him for a few minutes every day. However, if the pup starts to chew at the leash, simply keep it slack and let the pup choose where to go. The idea is to let your dog get the feel of the leash, but not get in the habit of chewing it. Repeat this a couple of times a day for two days, and the pup will get used to the leash without feeling restrained.

Next, you can let the pup understand that the leash will restrict his movements. The first time this happens, your dog will either pull, buck, or just sit down. Immediately call the pup to you and give him lots of praise. Never tug on the leash or drag the puppy along the floor. This might cause the puppy to associate his leash with negative consequences. After a few lessons, the puppy will be familiar with the restrictive feeling, and you can start going in a direction opposite from the pup. Give the leash a short tug so that the pup is brought to a halt, call the pup to you enthusiastically, and continue walking. When the puppy is walking happily on the leash, end the lesson with lots of praise. There is no rush for your puppy to learn leash training, so take as long as you need to make the dog feel comfortable.

BASIC COMMANDS

Although your puppy should attend puppy kindergarten, begin training as soon as your puppy is comfortable in your home and knows his name. It is also very helpful to take the lessons that you learn together in kindergarten and practice them at home. Doing your homework together will not only reinforce what you learn in class, it will allow you to spend some quality one-on-one time with your pup.

There are two very important things to remember when training your puppy. First, train the puppy without any potential distractions. Second, keep all lessons very short. Eliminating any distraction is important because it is essential that you have your puppy's full attention. This is not possible if there are other people, other dogs, butterflies, or birds to play with. Also, always remember that puppies have very short attention spans. Even when the pup has become a young adult, the maximum time you should train him would be about 20 minutes. However, you can give the puppy more than one lesson a day, three being as many as are recommended, each well apart. If you train any longer, the puppy will most likely become bored, and you will have to end the session on a down note, which you should never do.

Before beginning a lesson, always play a little game so that the puppy is in an active state of mind and more receptive to training. Likewise, always end lessons with play time for the pup, and always end training on a high note, praising the puppy. This will really build his confidence.

The Come Command

The come command is possibly the most important command you can teach your puppy—it may even save your dog's life someday. Knowing that your dog will come to you immediately when you call him will ensure that you can trust him to return to you if there is any kind of danger nearby. Teaching your puppy to come when called should always be a pleasant experience. You should never call your puppy in order to scold or yell at him or else he will soon learn not to respond.

For the best results, train your Brittany in a quiet, relaxing environment that is free of distractions.

When the pup comes to you, make sure to give him a lot of praise, petting, and, in the beginning, a treat. If he expects happy things when he reaches your side, you'll never have trouble getting your dog to come to you.

Start with your puppy on a long lead about 20 feet in length. Have plenty of treats that your puppy likes. Walk the distance of the lead, and then crouch down and say, "Come." Make sure that you use a happy, excited tone of voice when you call the pup's name. Your puppy should come to you enthusiastically. If not, use the long lead to pull him toward you, continuing to use the happy tone of voice. Give him lots of praise and a treat when you puppy gets there. Continue to use the long lead until your puppy is consistently obeying your command.

Once your Brittany can sit properly, teach him how to remain in position until you release him.

The Sit Command

As with most basic commands, your puppy will learn the sit command in just a few lessons. One 15-minute lesson each day should do the trick in no time. Some trainers will advise you that you should not proceed to other commands until the previous one has been learned really well. However, a bright young pup is quite capable of handling more than one command per lesson and certainly per day. As time progresses, you will be going through each command as a matter of routine before a new one is attempted. This is so the puppy always starts, as well as ends, a lesson on a high note, having successfully completed something.

There are two ways to teach the sit command. First, get a treat that your dog really likes and hold it right by his nose, so that all his attention is focused on it. Raise the treat above his head and say, "Sit." Usually, the puppy will follow the treat and automatically sit. Give him the treat for being such a good dog and don't forget to praise him. After a while, the pup will begin to associate the word "sit" with the action. Most puppies will catch on very quickly. Once your dog is sitting reliably with the treat, take it away and just use praise as a reward.

However, there are some puppies that are more stubborn than others. They may need a little more encouragement to get the picture. If your puppy doesn't sit automatically when the treat is over his head, place one hand on the pup's hindquarters and the other under his

Staying in one place can be very difficult for an energetic dog like the Brittany. Gently help your dog into position if he is having difficulty.

upper chest. Say, "Sit," in a pleasant (never harsh) voice, and at the same time, lightly push down on his rear end and push up under the chest until your dog is sitting. Give lots of praise and give the pup the treat. Repeat this a few times, and your pet will get the idea. Most puppies will also tend to stand up at first, so immediately repeat the exercise. When the puppy understands the command and does it right away, you can slowly move backward so that you are a few feet away. If he attempts to come to you, simply place the dog back in the original position and start again. Do not attempt to keep the pup in the sit position for too long. Even a few seconds is a long time for a impatient, energetic puppy, and you do

The down command can be challenging for some dogs to master because it puts them in a submissive position.

not want him to get bored with lessons before he has even begun them.

The Stay Command

The stay command should follow your sit lesson, but it can be very hard for puppies to understand. Remember that your puppy wants nothing more than to be at your side, so it will be hard for him to stay in one place while you walk away. You should only expect your dog to perform this command for a few seconds at first, and then gradually work up to longer periods of time.

Face the puppy and say, "Sit." Now step backward, saying, "Stay." It is also very helpful to use the hand signal for stay—place your hand straight out, palm toward the dog's nose. Let the pup remain in the position for only a few seconds before saying, "Come" and giving lots of praise and a treat. Once your dog gets the hang of it, repeat the command again, but step farther back. If the pup gets up and comes to you, simply go back to the original position and start again. As the pup starts to understand the command, you can move farther and farther back.

Once your puppy is staying reliably from a short distance, the next test is to walk away after placing the pup. This will mean your back is to the dog, which will tempt him to follow you. Keep an eye over your shoulder, and the minute the pup starts to move, spin around, say, "Stay," and start over from the original position.

As the weeks go by, you can increase the length of time the pup is left in the stay position—but two to three minutes is quite long enough for a puppy. If your puppy drops into a down position and is clearly more comfortable, there is nothing wrong with it. In the beginning, staying put is good enough!

The Down Command

From the puppy's viewpoint, the down command is one of the more difficult ones to accept. This position is submissive in a wild pack situation. A timid dog will roll over, which is a natural gesture of submission. A bolder pup will want to get up and might back off, not wanting to submit to this command. The dog will feel that he is about to be punished, which would be the position in a natural environment. Once he comes to understand this is not the case and that there are rewards for obeying, your pup will accept this position without any problem.

You may notice that some dogs will sit very quickly, but will respond to the down command more slowly. This is their way of saying that they will obey the command, but under protest!

There are two ways to teach this command. Obviously, with a puppy, it will be easier to teach the down if you are kneeling next to him. If your dog is more willing to please, the first method should work: Have your dog sit and hold a treat in front of his nose. When his full attention is on the treat, start to lower the treat slowly to the ground, saying, "Down." The pup should follow the treat with his head. Bring it out slowly in front

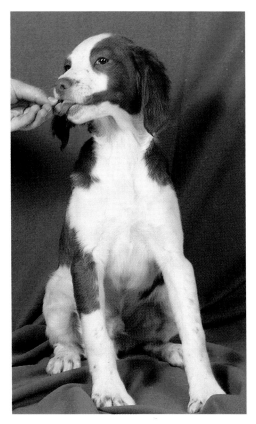

Use positive reinforcement to help your Brittany learn his commands, such as offering a treat for a job well done.

of him. If you are really lucky, your puppy will slide his legs forward and lie down by himself. Give the treat and lots of praise for being such a good dog. For a dog that won't lie down on his own (and most puppies won't), you can try this method: After the puppy is sitting and focused on the treat, take the front legs and gently sweep them forward, at the same time saying, "Down." Release the legs and quickly apply light pressure on the shoulders with your left hand. Then quickly tell the dog how good he is, give the treat, and make a lot of fuss. Repeat two or three times only in one training session. The pup will learn over a few lessons. Remember that this is a very submissive act on the pup's behalf, so there is no need to rush matters.

The Heel Command

All dogs should be able to walk nicely on a leash without a tug-of-war with their owners. Teaching your puppy the heel command should follow leash training. Heeling is best done in a place where you have a wall or a fence to one side of you, because it will restrict the puppy's movements so that you only have to contend with forward and backward situations. Again, it is better to do the lesson in private and not in a place where there will be many distractions.

There will be no need to use a slip collar on your puppy, as you can be just as effective with a flat, buckle one. The leash should be approximately 6 feet long. You can adjust the space between you, the puppy, and the wall so that your pet has only a small amount of room to move sideways. It is also very helpful to have a treat in your hand so that your dog will be focused on you and stay by your side.

Hold the leash in your right hand and pass it through your left. As the puppy moves ahead and pulls on the leash, give a quick jerk backward with your left hand, while at the same time saying, "Heel." You want the pup's head to be at, but not

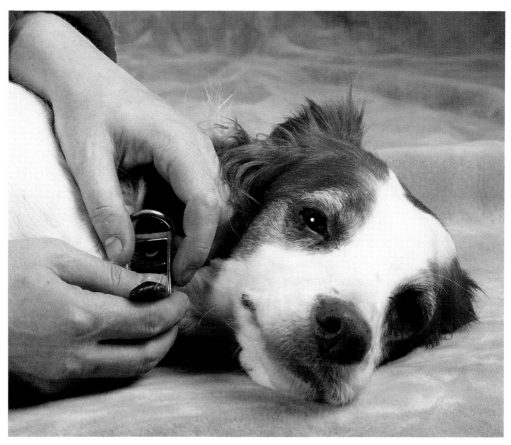

Make sure your dog wears his collar at all times for his safety.

THE GUIDE TO OWNING A BRITTANY

touching, your knee. When the puppy is in this position, praise him and begin walking again. Repeat the whole exercise. Once the puppy begins to get the message, you can use your left hand (with the treat inside of it) to pat the side of your knee so that the pup is encouraged to keep close to your side.

When the pup understands the basics, you can mix up the lesson a little to keep the dog focused. Do an about-turn, or make a quick left or right. This will result in a sudden jerk as you move in the opposite direction. The puppy will now be behind you, so you can pat your knee and say, "Heel." As soon as the pup is in the correct position, give him lots of praise. The puppy will now begin to associate certain words with certain actions. When not in the heel position, your dog will experience discomfort as you jerk the leash. When the pup is along side of you, he will receive praise. Given these two options, your dog will always prefer the praise.

Once the lesson is learned and the dog is heeling reliably, then you can change your pace from a slow walk to a quick one, and the puppy will come to adjust. The slow walk is always the more difficult for most puppies, as they are usually anxious to be on the move. End the lesson when the pup is walking nicely beside you. Begin the lesson with a few sit commands so you're starting with success and praise.

Recall to Heel Command

When your puppy is coming to the heel position from an off-leash situation—for

Most dogs have curious natures and like to explore their surroundings; however, their noses don't always lead them to the safest places. Teaching your Brittany the no command could keep him away from dangerous situations.

instance, if he has been running free—he should do this in the correct manner. He should pass behind you and take up his position, then sit. To teach this command, have the pup in front of you in the sit position with his collar and leash on. Hold the leash in your right hand. Give him the command to heel and pat your left knee. As the pup starts to move forward, use your right hand to guide him behind you. If you need to, you can hold the collar and walk the dog around the back of you to the desired position. You will need to repeat this a few times until the puppy understands what is wanted.

Brittanys are known for their athleticism and enjoy playing in the outdoors. There are many AKC field events in which your Brittany can participate and excel.

When you have done this a number of times, you can try it without the collar and leash. If the pup comes up toward your left side, then bring him to the sit position in front of you. Hold his collar and walk the pup around the back of you. Your dog will eventually understand and automatically pass around your back each time. If the dog is already behind you when you recall him, then the pup should automatically come to your left side. If necessary, pat your left leg.

The No Command

The no command must be obeyed every time. Your puppy must understand it 100 percent. Most delinquent dogs—the jumpers, the barkers, and the biters—have never been taught this command. If your puppy were to approach any potential danger, the no command, coupled with the come command, could save his life. You do not need a specific lesson for this command; it will most likely be used every day. You must be consistent and apply it every time your dog is doing something wrong. It is best, however, to be able to replace the negative command with something positive. This way, your puppy will respond quicker. For example, if your puppy is chewing on your shoe, tell him, "No!" and replace the shoe with a toy. Then give him lots of praise.

ADVANCED TRAINING

Once your Brittany has mastered the basic commands, you can put all his drive, stamina, and energy to good use while training him to do what he was bred to do. The American Kennel Club runs field trials and hunting tests that are open to pointing breeds—retrievers, spaniels, Basset Hounds, Beagles, and Dachshunds—over the age of six months that are registered with the AKC. Individual clubs sponsor these events under AKC sanctions or licenses. It is quite a thrill to see your Brittany develop and demonstrate his natural instincts.

In hunting tests, the dog's ability to perform is judged against a standard of perfection established by the AKC regulations. Dogs that receive qualifying scores at a number of tests achieve titles of JH (Junior Hunter), SH (Senior Hunter), and MH (Master Hunter), each successively requiring more skill.

In field trials, the dogs compete against each other for placements and points toward their championships. Successful dogs earn a FC (Field Champion) title in front of their name.

The field events are divided by subgroups of dogs and are sometimes limited to specific breeds. The Brittany is eligible to participate in pointing breed field trials and hunting tests. The dogs are run in braces around a course on which birds are released so that they can demonstrate their ability to find birds, point, and retrieve the downed birds.

There are many activities that the versatile Brittany can compete in. With a little hard work and patience, who knows how far your Brittany can go?

Your Healthy Brittany

Every Brittany puppy should be vaccinated against the major canine diseases. These are distemper, leptospirosis, hepatitis, and canine parvovirus. Your puppy may have received a temporary vaccination against distemper before you purchased him. Ask the breeder to be sure.

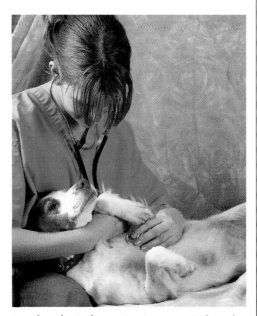

Regular physical examinations are vital to the health and long life of your canine companion.

The age at which vaccinations are given can vary, but will usually be when the pup is 8 to 12 weeks old. By this time, any protection given to the pup by antibodies received from his mother's initial milk feedings will be losing its strength.

The puppy's immune system works on the basis that the white blood cells engulf and render harmless attacking bacteria. However, they must first recognize a potential enemy.

Vaccines are either dead or alive bacteria in very small doses. Either type prompts the pup's defense system to attack them. When a large attack comes (if it does), the immune system recognizes it, and massive numbers of lymphocytes (white blood corpuscles) are mobilized to counter the attack. However, the ability of the cells to recognize these dangerous viruses can diminish over a period of time. It is therefore useful to provide annual reminders about the nature of the enemy. This is done by means of booster injections that keep the immune system on alert. Immunization is not a 100 percent guaranteed success in preventing illness, but it is very close. Certainly it is better than giving the puppy no protection.

Dogs are subject to other viral attacks. If there are high-risk factors in your area, your vet will suggest you have the puppy vaccinated against these as well.

Your puppy or dog should also be vaccinated against the deadly rabies virus. In fact, in many places it is illegal for your dog not to be vaccinated. This is to protect your dog, your family, and the rest of the animal population from this deadly virus that infects the nervous system and causes dementia and death.

GENERAL HEALTH

Dogs, like all other animals, are capable of contracting problems and diseases that, if listed, would seem overwhelming. However, in most cases, these are easily avoided by sound husbandry—well-bred and well-cared-for animals are less prone to developing diseases and problems than are carelessly bred and neglected animals. Your knowledge of how to avoid problems is far more valuable than all of the books and advice on how to cure them. Respectively, the only person you should listen to about treatment is your vet. Veterinarians don't have all the answers, but at least they are trained to analyze and treat illnesses, and are aware of the full implications of treatments,

By breeding only the best quality dogs, good health and temperament are passed down to each generation.

which most others are not. This does not mean a few old remedies aren't good standbys when all else fails. In most cases, modern science provides the best treatments for disease.

PHYSICAL EXAMS

Your puppy should receive regular physical examinations or checkups. These come in two forms. One is obviously performed by your vet, and the other is a day-to-day procedure that should be done by you. Apart from the fact that the exam will highlight any problem at an early stage, it is an excellent way of getting the pup used to being handled.

To do the physical exam yourself, start at the head and work your way around the

Brittanys enjoy time in the great outdoors.

body. You are looking for any sign of lesions or any indication of parasites on the pup. The most common parasites are fleas and ticks.

FIGHTING FLEAS

Fleas are very mobile and may be red, black, or brown in color. The adults suck the blood of the host, while the larvae feed on the adults' feces, which is rich in blood. Flea "dirt" may be seen on the pup as very tiny clusters of blackish specks that look like freshly ground pepper. The eggs of fleas may be laid on the puppy, though they are more commonly laid off the host in a more favorable place, such as the bedding. They normally hatch in 4 to

21 days, depending on the temperature, but they can survive for up to 18 months if temperature conditions are not favorable. The larvae are maggot-like and molt a couple of times before forming a pupae, which can survive long periods until the temperature or the vibration of a nearby host causes them to emerge.

There are a number of effective treatments available. Discuss them with your veterinarian, and then follow all instructions for the one that you choose. Any treatment will involve a product for your dog and one for the environment. This will require diligence on your part to treat all areas and thoroughly clean your home and yard until the infestation is eradicated.

THE TROUBLE WITH TICKS

Ticks are arthropods of the spider family, which means they have eight legs (though the larvae have six). They bury their headparts into the host and gorge on its blood. They are easily seen as small grain-like creatures sticking out from the skin. They are often picked up when dogs play in fields, but may also arrive in your yard via wild animals, birds, or stray cats and dogs. Some ticks are species-specific; others are more adaptable and will host on many species.

The most troublesome type of tick is the deer tick, which spreads the deadly Lyme disease that can cripple a dog (or a person). Deer ticks are tiny and very hard to detect. Often, by the time they're big enough to notice, they've been feeding on

There are many parasites, like fleas and ticks, that your Brittany may encounter while playing outside. Be sure to check his coat thoroughly when he comes in from the outdoors.

the dog for a few days—long enough to do their damage. Lyme disease was named for the area in which it was first detected—Lyme, Connecticut—but has now been diagnosed in almost all parts of the US. Your veterinarian can advise you of the danger to your dog(s) in your area, and may suggest your dog be vaccinated for Lyme. Always go over your dog with a fine-toothed flea comb when you come in from walking through any area that may harbor deer ticks. If your dog is acting unusually sluggish or sore, seek veterinary advice.

Attempts to pull a tick free will invariably leave the headpart in the pup, where it will die and cause an infected wound or abscess. The best way to remove ticks is to dab a strong saline solution, iodine, or alcohol on them. This will numb them, causing them to loosen their hold, at which time they can be removed with tweezers. The wound can then be cleaned and covered with an antiseptic ointment. If ticks are common in your area, consult with your vet for a suitable pesticide to be used in kennels, on bedding, and on the dog.

If your Brittany does a lot of hunting or spends a lot of time outdoors, there are other insects and outdoor dangers of which you must be careful. There are many biting insects, such as mosquitoes, that can cause discomfort or transmit diseases to your Brittany.

A Brittany can easily get a grass seed or thorn lodged between his pads or in the folds of his ears. These may go unnoticed until an abscess forms. Your daily check of your dog will do a world of good. If your puppy has been playing in long grass or places where there may be thorns, pine needles, wild animals, or parasites, the checkup is a wise precaution.

SKIN DISORDERS

Apart from problems associated with lesions created by biting pests, a puppy may fall foul to a number of other skin disorders, such as ringworm, mange, and eczema. Ringworm is not caused by a worm, but is a fungal infection. It manifests itself as a sore-looking bald circle. If your puppy has any form of bald patches, let your veterinarian check him over; a microscopic examination can confirm the condition. Many old remedies for ringworm exist, such as iodine, carbolic acid, formalin, and other tinctures, but modern drugs are superior.

Fungal infections can be very difficult to treat, and even more difficult to eradicate, because of the spores. These can withstand most treatments, other than burning, which is the best thing to do with bedding once the condition has been confirmed.

Mange is a general term that can be applied to many skin conditions where the hair falls out and a flaky crust develops and falls away.

Often, dogs will scratch themselves, and this invariably is worse than the original condition, for it opens lesions that are then subject to viral, fungal, or parasitic attack. The cause of the problem

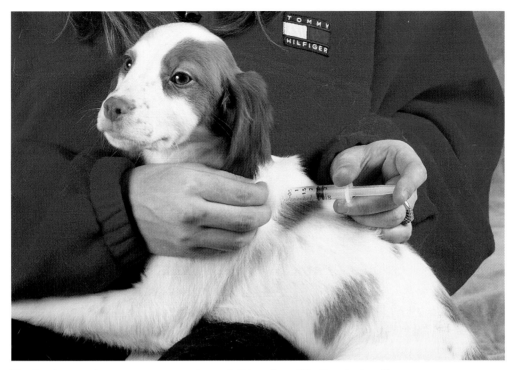
Vaccinations are important to protect your Brittany from life-threatening diseases.

can be various species of mites. These either live on skin debris and the hair follicles, which they destroy, or they bury themselves just beneath the skin and feed on the tissue. Applying general remedies from pet stores is not recommended because it is essential to identify the type of mange before a specific treatment is effective.

Eczema is another non-specific term applied to many skin disorders. The condition can be brought about in many ways. Sunburn, chemicals, allergies to foods, drugs, and pollens—even stress— can all produce a deterioration of the skin and coat. Given the range of causal factors, treatment can be difficult because the problem is one of identification. It is a case of taking each possibility at a time and trying to correctly diagnose the matter. If the cause is dietary in nature, you must remove one item at a time in order to find out if the dog is allergic to a given food. It could, of course, be the lack of a nutrient that is the problem, so if the condition persists, you should consult your veterinarian.

WORMS

There are many species of worms, and a number of these live in the tissues of dogs and most other animals. Many create no problem at all, so you are not even aware they exist. Others can be tolerated in small levels, but become a major problem if they number more than a few. The most common types seen in dogs are round-worms and tapeworms. While round-worms are the greater problem, tapeworms require an intermediate host so they are more easily eradicated.

Roundworms of the species *Toxocara canis* infest the dog. They may grow to a length of 8 inches (20 cm) and look like strings of spaghetti. The worms feed on the digesting food in the pup's intestines. In chronic cases the puppy will become pot-bellied, have diarrhea and will vomit. Having passed through a stage when he always seems hungry, eventually, he will stop eating. The worms lay eggs in the puppy that pass out in his feces. They are then either ingested by the pup, or are eaten by mice, rats, or beetles. The puppy may then eat these and the life cycle is complete.

Larval worms can migrate to the womb of a pregnant bitch or to her mammary glands, and this is how they pass to the puppy. The pregnant bitch can be wormed, which will help. The pups can, and should, be wormed when they are about two weeks old. Repeat worming every 10 to 14 days and the parasites should be removed. Worms can be extremely dangerous to young puppies, so you should be sure the pup is wormed as a matter of routine.

Tapeworms can be seen as tiny rice-like eggs sticking to the puppy or dog's anus. They are less destructive, but still undesirable. The eggs are eaten by mice, fleas, rabbits, and other animals that serve as intermediate hosts. They develop into a larval stage and must be eaten by the dog in order to complete the chain. Your vet will supply a suitable remedy if tapeworms are seen or suspected. The vet can also do an egg count on the pup's feces under the microscope; this will indicate the extent of an infestation.

There are other worms, such as hookworms and whipworms, that are also bloodsuckers. They will make a pup anemic, and blood might be seen in the feces, which can be examined by the vet to confirm their presence. Cleanliness in all matters is the best preventative measure for all worms.

BLOAT (GASTRIC DILATATION)

This condition has proved fatal in many dogs, especially large and deep-chested breeds, such as the Rottweiler or the Great Dane. However, any dog can get bloat. It is caused when gases build up in the stomach, especially in the small intestine. Carbohydrates are fermented and release gases. Normally, these gases are released by belching or by being passed from the anus. If for any reason these exits become blocked (such as if the stomach twists due to physical exertion), the gases cannot escape and the stomach simply swells and places pressure on other organs, sometimes cutting off the blood supply to the heart or causing suffocation. Death can easily follow if the condition goes undetected.

The best preventative measure is not to feed large meals or exercise your puppy or dog immediately after he has eaten. You can reduce the risk of flatulence by feeding more fiber in the diet, not feeding too many dry biscuits, and possibly by adding activated charcoal tablets to the diet.

ACCIDENTS

All puppies will get their share of bumps and bruises due to the rather energetic way they play. These will usually rectify themselves over a few days. Small cuts should be bathed with a suitable disinfectant and then smeared with an antiseptic ointment. If a cut looks more serious, stem the flow of blood with a towel or makeshift tourniquet, and rush the pup to the veterinarian. Never apply too much pressure to the wound as it might restrict the flow of blood to the limb.

In the case of burns, you should apply cold water or an ice pack to the surface. If the burn was due to a chemical then this must be washed away with copious amounts of water. Apply petroleum jelly, or any vegetable oil, to the burn. Trim away the hair if need be. Wrap the dog in a blanket and rush him to the vet. The pup may go into shock, depending on the severity of the burn, resulting in a lowered blood pressure, which is dangerous and the reason the pup must receive immediate veterinary attention.

If a broken limb is suspected, try to keep the animal as still as possible. Wrap your pup or dog in a blanket to restrict movement and get him to the veterinarian as soon as possible. Do not move the dog's head so it is tilting backward, as this might result in blood entering the lungs.

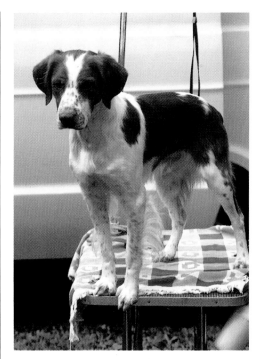

Keep a watchful eye on your Brittany while he is on the grooming table. A fall could cause considerable injury.

Do not let your pup jump up and down from heights, as this can cause considerable shock to the joints. Like all youngsters, puppies do not know when enough is enough, so you must do all their thinking for them.

Provided you apply strict hygiene to all aspects of your puppy's husbandry, and you make daily checks on his physical state, you have done as much as you can to safeguard him during his most vulnerable period. Routine visits to your veterinarian are also recommended, especially while the puppy is under one year of age. The vet may notice something that did not seem important to you.

Index

Photo Credits

All photos by Isabelle Francais